WILLOW TREE

a poem by

Harriet Ribot

Finishing Line Press
Georgetown, Kentucky

WILLOW TREE

Publisher: Leah Huete de Maines
Editor: Christen Kincaid
Cover Art: Dale Erickson
Author Photo: from Family Collection
Cover Design: Elizabeth Maines McCleavy

Order online: www.finishinglinepress.com
also available on amazon.com

Author inquiries and mail orders:
Finishing Line Press
PO Box 1626
Georgetown, Kentucky 40324
USA

To all who brought me to maturity—

i.

Branches topped with snow
against a sky of gray
beneath which
newly fallen snow lay.
Slowly the sky turns to blue.
Between branches, sun filters through
as snow plows and motors
erupt in the dawn,
voices intrude, as does a horn.
Into the morning
cacophony is borne.

High above the willow tree,
from your window, I can see
shadows reach
and fade as they go
about their business
in the house
beyond the shades.
Through this window
I see dreams take shape
from memory
turning, gliding, rising free,
like cardinals' wings in flight
held firmly in my sight.

Caressed by March's moisture,
wind borne whippets,
precursor of a summer past,
stretch toward spring.
Straw-colored branches remain—
a fantasy of prancing horses
disappear into a sea of blue,
abandoning their willow tails.

ii.

Willow tree—
there it stands.
March winds
coax boughs
clean and spare
as a whippet
straining
at the starting gate.

The warm rays
of the sun's
benevolence
release a yellow haze
enveloping this gift of nature.
Angel wings
of green evolve,
playful guardians
of their host
until summer bids
the boughs
at ease.

iii

Bare branches soon unveil
a profusion of tightly knit buds.

Roughed up by high winds,
branches cross each other—

a seemingly hopeless tangle,
but time has a way

of straightening some things out.
Growing leaves soon lend weight

to protect the slender branches
from being buffeted

by each whim of nature.

iv.

Spring moves in rapidly. Color drifts softly into grasses,
to the willow tree, and a strongly pigmented spruce.

Armadas of dandelion seeds launch from their stems, waft
    through space and trees,
like spaceships from many galaxies engaged in combat. Then,

steered by an unseen captain, change direction upward and down
again to earth. Thousands of seeds move toward the willow tree
    and hover

mid-air, intimidated by the swaying willow branches: paired
    leaves
not fully developed along each tapered branch, a formation

of butterflies in flight. The mini-missiles, directed by an updraft
swerve and quickly penetrate the tree while its branches belatedly

whip about, scattering the invaders.

v.

Now, I see wisteria leaning
against a willow tree,
its green leaves
bobbing in a lavender sea—
alien beauty on a stalwart willow,
seeking solace on its pillow
in a stretch toward spring,
tired of March's slings.

vi.

If they asked about you I would say
through your window I see many things—
clouds resting in the sky
dark or light, or drifting by.
Bumble bees and spring and winter,
serigraphed in one short hour
stretched out over days, 'come seasons
blue jays turn on gusts of wind
harsh to even willow trees,
defying limbs at ease.

Through your window in surprise
a daytime moon begins to rise.
Passing birds with outspread wings
or even those just hovering
uncertain of their destination—
a portion of its flight our ration,
seen between the window frames.

vii.

I see shadows in the house below
leading lives I do not know.
Wondering, if in their view,
I'm a shadow too.
Invisible to them, divisible to me:
one side wants to be held,
the other to be free.

Why look out if not to find something—
I come here searching, three times weekly.
Like paintings by Utrillo
following a narrow street to a distant church
to seek what I might reach, but never know.

Now the willow's leaves resemble
pigtails sporting a tie
which pirouette with any
slight breeze. A reminder that
soon we'll say goodbye.

viii.

You've taken strands from tales I've told
braided them into a crown
to let me view all sides of it, and
on my head you set it down
—to go forth in my own realm.

ix.

Raised by Nature's graces,
downed by her truculence
wrenched by a wind storm,
it rests like a felled giant,
tresses back,
roots extended,
a hairy great foot
covered by moss.
The carnage of its
dismembered branches
strewn about.

The intrusion of chainsaws
hasten removal of an inert
slash across the landscape.

Silently, earth and the brook
absorb the sawdust.

Harriet Ribot grew up in Brighton Beach, Brooklyn, in the 1930s and 40s. Her father made eyeglass frames in New York after leaving the Austro-Hungarian Empire at age seventeen. Her mother, from the same region, came over at sixteen, and found work as a trimmer for an American flag factory. Ribot is the youngest of three siblings. After a lifelong habit of keeping journals, which she called, "conversations with myself," and after her own children (four boys) were grown, she enrolled in Rutgers-Newark, where she earned a BA in English with a concentration in Journalism in 1985. Three professors in the English Department encouraged her to release her creative energies and to continue to write poems and essays. Close to four decades later, she is ready to share those efforts.

www.ingramcontent.com/pod-product-compliance
Lightning Source LLC
Chambersburg PA
CBHW031907110426
R18126200001B/R181262PG42743CBX00004B/1